I SEE ANIMAL TEXTURES!

SHELLS

by Jenna Lee Gleisner

TABLE OF CONTENTS

tadpole books

WORDS TO KNOW

bumpy

shell

smooth

spiral

spotted

striped

SHELLS

shell

I see a shell.

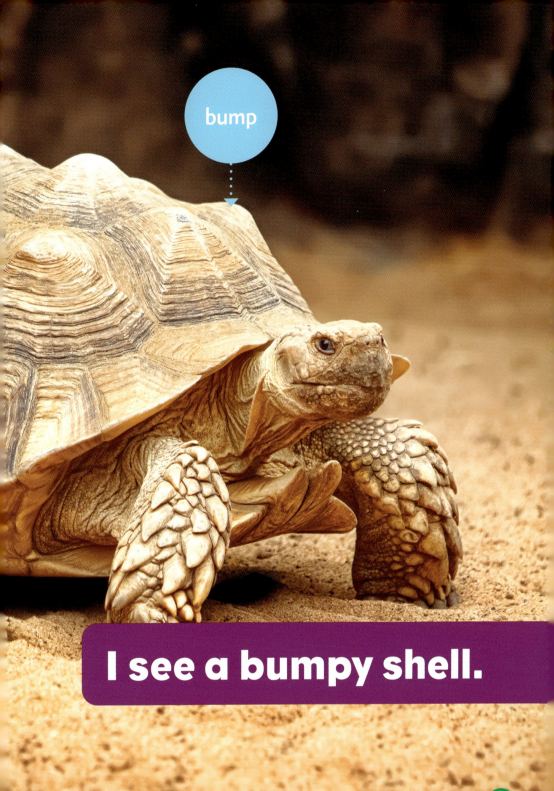

bump

I see a bumpy shell.

5

I see a smooth shell.

spot

I see a spotted shell.

stripe

I see a striped shell.

11

spiral

I see a spiral shell.

shell

I see a small shell!

15

LET'S REVIEW!

Animals with soft bodies have shells. Shells keep animals safe. They can also live in them. What kinds of shells do you see below?

INDEX